bubblefacts...

VICTORIAN TIMES

Miles Kelly
PUBLISHING

First published in 2006 by
Miles Kelly Publishing Ltd
Bardfield Centre, Great Bardfield, Essex, CM7 4SL

Copyright © Miles Kelly Publishing Ltd 2006

2 4 6 8 10 9 7 5 3 1

Publishing Director:
Anne Marshall

Senior Editor:
Belinda Gallagher

Art Director:

Designer:

Cartoons:
Mark Davis

Production:
Elizabeth Brunwin

ISBN 1-84236-657-2

Reprographics: Mike Coupe, Stephan Davis

Printed in China

British Library Cataloguing-in-Publication Data
A catalogue record for this book is available from the British Library

Indexer: Jane Parker

www.mileskelly.net
info@mileskelly.net

Contents

4 *Queen of an empire*
a new era

6 *Richer or poorer?*
it's a hard life

8 *Work and no play*
job search

10 *Wicked workhouses*
a miserable life

12 *Bright ideas*
clever clogs!

14 *Keep on moving*
getting around

16 *And... relax*
winding down

18 *Doctor, doctor...*
medical marvels

20 *Building blocks*
great architects

22 *Glorious food*
dinner time!

24 *You're nicked!*
law and order

26 *School rules*
teacher's pet!

28 *Family life*
home sweet home

30 *Telling tales*
great authors

32 *Index*

Queen of an empire
a new era

Queen Victoria came to the throne in 1837. During her 54-year reign, Britain was transformed by the Industrial Revolution. It became the most powerful nation in the world. The rich became richer than they could ever have dreamed of, but the poor faced terrible poverty.

A-TEN-SHUN!

LEFT HOLDING THE BABY.

WAH! WAH!

YES! YES! YES!

HAVEN'T ASKED YOU YET.

Victoria's father died when she was a baby. She became queen at 18 and married Prince Albert in 1840.

Victoria and Albert had a happy marriage, and they had nine children. Their names were Vicky, Edward, Alice, Alfred, Helena, Louise, Arthur, Leopold and Beatrice.

British law stated that no man was allowed to propose to the queen, so Victoria had to ask for Albert's hand in marriage!

Victoria and Albert valued family life. Unfortunately, three of their children died before Victoria did.

Richer or poorer?

it's a hard life

The poor lived in tiny, dirty terraced houses. They rarely had running water and one house was often home to a family of ten. For the rich, Victorian Britain was a wonderful place to live. They wore expensive clothes and went to the theatre.

Poor families had to live in cramped, dirty conditions. Brothers and sisters had to share a bed.

People began to demand the right to vote. In the 1840s in Ireland, thousands died from starvation.

The rich wore fabulous clothes and expensive jewellery. They flocked to musicals and lavish events.

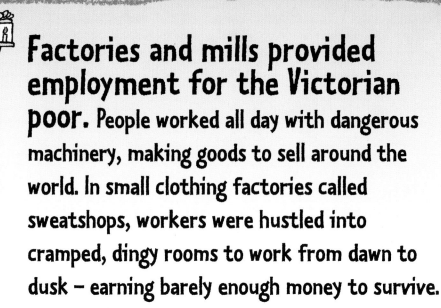

Work and no play

job search

Factories and mills provided employment for the Victorian poor. People worked all day with dangerous machinery, making goods to sell around the world. In small clothing factories called sweatshops, workers were hustled into cramped, dingy rooms to work from dawn to dusk – earning barely enough money to survive.

By the 1850s printing had been mechanized. Mining was one of the deadliest jobs in Victorian Britain.

Miners faced the constant threat of unstable shafts and explosive gases. To check for gas, miners often took canaries to work with them. If the birds stopped singing, it was seen as a sign that gas was present. In 1842 the Mines Act was passed, banning children from working in mines.

SWEEP THAT CHIMNEY SHARPISH!

RING!

APPLES AND PEARS...

DING!

WHAT'RE YOU SELLING? STAIRS?

SWEAT!!

oys were sent up chimneys to sweep them clean. Pedlars tried to sell their wares, such as rags, on the street.

Wicked workhouses

a miserable life

Workhouses were supposed to encourage the poor to be less reliant on hand-outs. So in order to receive poor relief, such as food or clothes, people had to live in workhouses. The conditions in these places were terrible. People were starving and cold, and children were often beaten.

Food in the workhouse consisted of watery soup called gruel, and a little bread and cheese.

The writer Charles Dickens was so shocked by the conditions of workhouses that he wrote *Oliver Twist* to highlight the problem. Dickens campaigned throughout his lifetime to turn public opinion against these terrible places.

Rich ladies wore corsets made of whalebone, strengthened with steel! These gave them a tiny waist but must have been agony to wear.

WHEN I GET OUT OF HERE...

I'LL KNOCK HIS BLOCK OFF!

YIKES!!

CHILDREN SHOULD BE SEEN AND NOT HEARD.

SO SHOULD SOME ADULTS!

Children were beaten for misbehaving and many ended up in hospital as a result of their punishment.

Bright ideas

clever clogs!

CAN'T YOU KNOCK FIRST?

The Victorians were full of clever ideas. Prince Albert was so impressed with these ideas and inventions that he decided to hold the Great Exhibition to show them off. In 1851 thousands of people gathered in the newly built Crystal Palace to show off their gadgets to the dazzled public.

I MADE IT ALL BY MYSELF.

CLEVER BOY!

CREEP!

Crystal Palace was three times the length of St Paul's cathedral and covered 26 acres.

William Cook and Charles Wheatstone invented the Victorian internet – the electric telegraph. In 1837 they started to send messages down metal lines using electricity. In 1866 telegraph lines were laid under the Atlantic Ocean all the way to Canada.

Can you believe it?

The Victorian Age also saw the first dentist's drill and the first porcelain false teeth!

OOCH! OUCH!

ZZ ZZ!!

BLING!

EUREKA!

YOU SOUND LIKE A BABE!

YOU CHARMER! BET YOU'RE GORGEOUS TOO!

Swan invented the lightbulb in 1860, and the telephone arrived in 1876. Photography also became popular.

Keep
on moving
getting around

Victorian steam trains hurtled along tracks. By 1900, 35,000 kilometres of track had been laid in Britain. One of the most famous routes ran from the West Country to London and was designed by Isambard Kingdom Brunel (1806–1859). Passengers were so impressed that the railway was nicknamed 'God's Wonderful Railway'.

HORSE PLAY!

WHEN I SAID LUXURY TRAIN I MEANT ORIENT EXPRESS!

WISH I'D BROUGHT MY SAILOR'S OUTFIT!

PUFF! PUFF! PUFF!

Brunel also designed *The Great Western*, the biggest ship in the world of its time. It reached the USA in 183?

Some people thought that travelling on the fastest Victorian trains would lead to death by suffocation!

Isambard Kingdom Brunel was a brilliant engineer. He is famous for his designs of railways, bridges, tunnels and great ocean liners. *The Great Western* was the first steamship to take part in transatlantic service. Brunel went on to design two more great steamships – *The Great Britain* and *The Great Eastern*.

In 1853, George Cayley flew a glider 200 metres. The first practical cars appeared in 1895.

And... *relax*

winding down

Thanks to the arrival of railways, holidays became available to the Victorian public. People loved trips to the seaside, and resorts such as Blackpool and Brighton became popular holiday spots. Educated young men and women travelled abroad to places such as Switzerland and Italy, visiting sights such as Mount Vesuvius.

Wealthy people used bathing machines. These were horse-drawn huts that were wheeled into the sea.

People in towns and cities loved going to music halls. These were large rooms built at the side of pubs. Here, people could watch simple plays, or entertainers such as singers and dancers. Marie Lloyd was one of the most famous entertainers and was given the nickname Queen of the Music Hall.

WHOOSSHHHHH!

HE'S A BUNDLE OF LAUGHS!

HANDBALL! REF!

FLYING TRUNK! LOOK OUT!

...e professional football league was formed. Tossing the caber (tree trunk) was part of the Highland Games.

In 1867 Joseph Lister invented a spray that could kill germs.
Lister realized that many deaths in hospitals were caused by infection during surgery. Carbolic acid spray killed these germs and deaths fell from 45 percent to 15 percent.

Operating theatres became much cleaner and safer with the use of carbolic acid spray.

In 1847 Doctor John Snow began using a chemical called chloroform in the operating theatre. This put patients into a deep sleep and stopped them feeling any pain during surgery. For hundreds of years patients had died on the operating table from shock. In 1853, Queen Victoria used the drug during the birth of Prince Leopold.

Chloroform put patients into a deep sleep. This meant people didn't experience pain during surgery.

Building blocks

great architects

'Gothic' was a style of architecture very popular in Victorian times. Buildings with pointed arches and high spires sprung up all over the land. The most famous examples of Gothic architecture are the new Houses of Parliament, the University of Glasgow and St Pancras station in London.

The new Houses of Parliament replaced the Palace of Westminster when it burned down in 1834.

The Victorians loved to build with iron and glass. Iron bridges spanned rivers, such as the Forth Rail Bridge in Scotland. Probably the most famous iron and glass building was the Crystal Palace, which housed the Great Exhibition in 1851.

Greek-style architecture became popular in Scotland. Four churches were built in this style by Alexander 'Greek' Thomson.

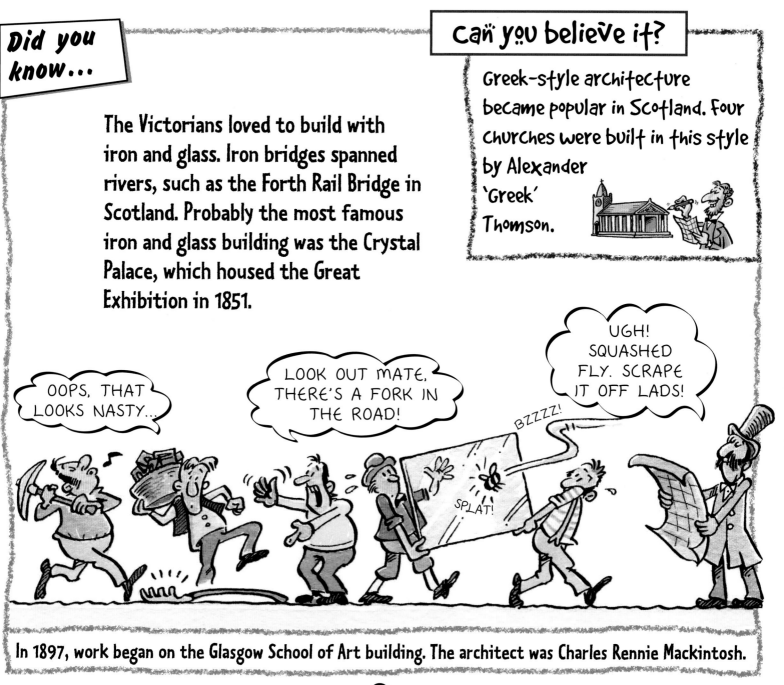

In 1897, work began on the Glasgow School of Art building. The architect was Charles Rennie Mackintosh.

Glorious food

dinner time!

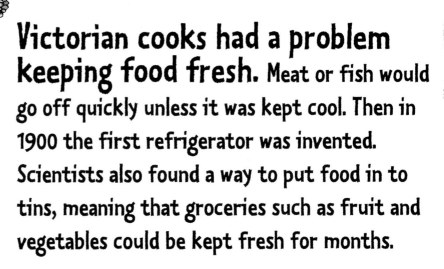

Victorian cooks had a problem keeping food fresh. Meat or fish would go off quickly unless it was kept cool. Then in 1900 the first refrigerator was invented. Scientists also found a way to put food in to tins, meaning that groceries such as fruit and vegetables could be kept fresh for months.

Cooks worked very hard. All food was prepared by hand. The arrival of ice cream delighted children!

Exotic fruits such as pineapple and kiwi were enjoyed by the wealthy. Spices from India became popular.

Milkmen carried large pails of milk, which was delivered straight from the farm to people's doors.

You're nicked!

law and order

By 1856, most towns and cities had their own police force. The first policemen were known as 'peelers' or 'bobbies'. This was after Sir Robert Peel, who set up London's Metropolitan police force in 1829. Policemen had wooden truncheons to help defend themselves against criminals.

FINDERS KEEPERS!

OI! GET BACK HERE, YOU TEA LEAF!

FINE MESS THIS IS!

GULP!

Policemen wore blue tailcoats and reinforced top hats. This helped people to recognize them.

In 1884 fingerprints were first used to identify criminals. Soon after, detectives learned how to spot tiny specks of blood. There were also new methods for detecting the use of poison, one of the most common forms of murder.

People were so gripped by Sir Arthur Conan Doyle's stories about the detective Sherlock Holmes, they thought he was real!

Science helped to solve crimes – but pickpockets were still rife. Fewer people were sentenced to death.

School rules

teacher's pet!

In 1880 a new law meant that all children between the ages of five and ten had to go to school. However, education wasn't free, so few children could afford to attend. Then in 1891 the law was changed, and school became free for all children up to the age of 11.

Lessons focused on the 'three Rs' – Reading, wRiting and aRithmetic. Children learned by repeating lines.

Many working-class children had to work all week, and had little chance to learn. Sunday or Charity Schools were set up to try to give these children a basic education. They were taught how to read and write and they also attended Bible study classes.

The most famous pickpocket is the Artful Dodger, a character in Dickens' novel *Oliver Twist*.

OOPS! NO SHOES!

SORRY WE'RE LATE!

DING! DING!

DETENTION FOR YOU TWO!

THE SHAME OF IT!

If a pupil was poor at a lesson, they would have to stand in a corner and wear the dunce's cap.

Family life
home sweet home

Home life was important to the Victorians. Home was a place to relax, and have dinner and entertain friends. Wealthy families would gather round the fire to play games, listen to the piano or tell stories. Working-class families spent their leisure time elsewhere because their homes were often dingy and cramped.

Poor families would eat from cheap food stalls. Everyone loved crowding round the piano for a sing-song.

Naughty children were not tolerated. Rich parents employed nannies to care for their children.

Children had toys such as hobby horses and yo-yos. They also played games such as snakes and ladders.

Telling tales

great authors

The most famous storyteller in Victorian Britain was Charles Dickens. He was fascinated by the poor areas of London and would pound the streets at night, making notes of what he saw. The Brontë sisters went on to become some of the greatest writers of the Victorian age.

Perhaps Dickens, most famous novel is *Oliver Twist*. The Brontës were raised on the bleak Yorkshire Moors.

When Queen Victoria died, people wore black. Iron fences were given a fresh coat of black paint, too.

Robert Louis Stevenson could write with astonishing speed. The scottish novelist wrote *The Strange Case of Doctor Jekyll and Mr Hyde* – a story of a troubled doctor who turns into Mr Hyde, a nasty character, after drinking a potion. Stevenson also wrote *Treasure Island* and *Kidnapped*, all about pirate adventures.

Robert Louis Stevenson wrote several famous novels. *Alice in Wonderland* was written by Lewis Carroll.

Index

A
Albert, Prince 4, 5, 12
Alice in Wonderland 31
architecture 20, 21

B
bathing machines 16
bridges 15, 21
Brontë sisters 30
Brunel, I. K. 14, 15

C
Carroll, Lewis 31
cars 15
chimney sweeps 9
Cook, William 13
Crystal Palace 12, 21

D
dentists 13
Dickens, C. 11, 27, 30
Doyle, Arthur C. 25

E
education 26, 27
employment 8

F
factories 8
Forth Rail Bridge 21
funfairs 17

G
games 28, 29
Great Exhibition 12, 21

H
Highland Games 17
holidays 16
Holmes, Sherlock 25
Houses of Parliament 20

I
Industrial Revolution 4
inventions 12, 13

L
lessons 26, 27
Lister, Joseph 18
Lloyd, Marie 17

M
Mackintosh, C. R. 21
Metropolitan Police Force 24
mining 8, 9
music halls 17

N
Nightingale, Florence 9

O
Oliver Twist 11, 27, 30
operating theatres 18, 19

P
pedlars 9
Peel, Sir Robert 24

photography 13
pickpockets 25, 27
police forces 24
poor 6, 8, 10, 28
printing 8

R
railways 14, 15, 16

S
school 26, 27
scientists 22
seaside 16
ships 14, 15
Snow, Dr John 19
St Pancras station 20
steam power 14, 15, 17
Stevenson, R. L. 31
Sunday School 27
surgery 18, 19
sweatshops 8

T
telegraph 13
telephone 13
theatre 6
Thomson, A. 21
toys 29
trains 14, 15
Treasure Island 31

V
Victoria, Queen 4, 5, 19, 31

W
Wheatstone, C. 13
workhouses 10, 11